# LIZA HAYNES

# "Piece of Cake" Party Planning

*An Easy Guide to Planning an Event Big or Small*

First edition

This book was professionally typeset on Reedsy.
Find out more at reedsy.com

*To my husband and my kids, my heart beats for you.*

# Contents

# 1

# Introduction:

*"Let Them Eat Cake" - Marie-Antoinette*

Welcome to my simple and easy party planning guide. It has been a dream of mine for some time to write a quick hand book about one of my passions in life… party/event planning. I'm a married mom of 2, and from the time that my oldest (now 15) was a baby like every other mom I was envisioning his 1st birthday party. Honestly I didn't know where to start. I just knew that I was extremely enthusiastic to get it planned and as the weeks went on not only did I realize that I took pleasure in it, I noticed that I had a knack for it.

I really did not know where to begin so I started researching ideas, venues, themes, food, games etc…..and I ended up on the theme Little Einsteins which back in 2009 was a highly famous Disney show for little ones. The party turned out wonderful and virtually everything went as planned and of course my 1 yr old son could care less about it all, he was just happy eating his cake! I did make a few mistakes but in the end I would consider it a success.

As the years progressed every year was a fresh theme, and a brand new idea and then the holidays would come and I would have an entirely new and different party to plan and research for and before I knew it my daughter was born, more planning and more parties…and now almost 16 years later I have done just about every kind of event/party. I've done funerals, weddings, 50yr birthday bashes, ALL the kids birthday parties with every kind of theme (including a dragon theme by turning my front entrance hallway into a cave with brown butcher paper), and I've even done a Louisiana Style Crab Bake!!!

In 2016 I decided I wanted to be more knowledgeable and so I attended the New York Institute of Art and Design and was certified as an Event Planner. I thoroughly enjoyed myself in all of the courses that I took. I savored the barrage of information I was receiving, it was fantastic. When I was done I had learned a great deal and I had a fire in me to do more. In this book I am going to give you the basics on how to throw a party, big or small, elegant or casual and some secrets and tips for making it very cost effective and simple.

You can expect to gain new knowledge and understand to not be intimidated or overwhelmed by it, it can actually be enjoyable and pleasing. Yes, some events are more involved and require a lot more attention to detail then others, for instance a wedding but the same principles apply to every event they just change depending on the size and type of event. What I want you to remember is that organization and having fun with it is key.

INTRODUCTION:

With all that being said let's jump right in!!

# 2

# Let's Get It Started

For the highest level of success I am going to recommend that you keep some kind of binder or notebook to keep you on track and to keep all of your planning information and ideas in that binder. In this chapter we will cover the budget, the venue, the theme and the invites. The first order of business that you need to decide on is the budget, yes that nasty word budget. It would be a dream to not have to have a budget and I know it's not something we want to think about but it is KEY to your event and it is the master control of how you will plan the rest of the event. In the case of a large event or a more significant event like a wedding or a quinceanera you will want to make an excel spreadsheet to keep track of everything and what things are costing so you can keep track of your spending. It is important to make sure you have columns eg. venue, food, flowers etc...for all the things that you will need to pay for and be sure to input all the amounts as the quotes or invoices come in. Of course when we are talking about casual birthday parties, or say a retirement party or even a fancy BBQ you don't have to be so professional although you will still need to have a place where you make notes. You will need to be certain that you have created a timeline so that you are able to coordinate all aspects of the event which would include entertainment, vendor arrival, meal time etc. This is vital to keeping the flow of the event moving smoothly and staying on track.

Once you have established your budget your next order of business is how many people you will invite, this is critical because that number will dictate the venue you choose. Again the budget matters because you will need to make sure the venue you choose is in your budget. Of course if this is for a children's party or something basic you still need to figure out how many people you're inviting because maybe your "backyard" can not accommodate that number of guests. It's essential that you have enough room for people to mingle and have a place to sit down and eat comfortably.

When it comes to the guest count, if you are planning a wedding it is imperative that you get as close to knowing how many guests are expected as possible, we will talk about that in a moment. For a child's party or a casual event you can estimate how many people based on the invites you send out. We all know that when it comes to a casual event not everyone that says they will be attending actually shows up so you can make adjustments for that because it is a casual event.

Next, you will be selecting the theme for the event. You can go online and research many ideas for different themes and decor. You may already have an idea in your head and that is fantastic because you will have a starting point. However, if you do not there are many places to get inspiration and a creative concept from. I do really like Etsy, and Pinterest. They are a fabulous resource for ideas. The theme of an event plays a large role , it actually is the biggest role of all. The theme you choose will decide the style or the "feel"l of the event. Your decor should all tie in together to that one central idea. Have fun with it, a theme can almost always be dressed up or dressed down and let your imagination go wild with ideas of how to decorate the space. You always want your guests to feel welcomed and to take pleasure in their time at your event so much so that they don't realize how fast the time is going.

If the venue you pick is not the exact decor that you want, don't be alarmed; you can always *zhuzh* it up to make it what you want it to be! When picking your venue all locations will include the ceremony space, a lounging area and usually 2 separate locations for wedding parties to get ready in. They may also include the meal, the linen and often the cake will be included in the price of the site as well. Most venues work with specific caterers and florists etc…so it becomes less complicated for you because they will be able to get you in touch with the vendors they already know and trust and they normally have a wedding coordinator who will be your main contact.

Once you pick your theme you can then decide on what kind of places work best. For example for a wedding or a formal event you will want to find a location that has the space for all of your guests and you will want to have an idea as to how you want the event to look. Do you want inside or outside, do you want lots of greenery or do you want it by the beach? These are all factors to take into consideration. You will have to do some research, some venues have sites specifically for outside use while others have sites for inside events. Once you have a concept as to the look and the vibe of the event make a few appointments to visit a few sites you are interested in, I can tell you that usually the moment you step into a certain venue you will know it IS the place you want. But also sometimes you may have to be flexible because something else may be conflicting… like the budget. The key is keep your options versatile and be open minded.

When it comes to a less formal event, decisions are simpler and considerably less complicated. For example, maybe for your daughter's birthday party she would like to do a farm animal theme, so you might look for a location that has a petting zoo or if you have it in your budget you may be able to bring the petting zoo to you! Or perhaps for an 80's themed party you can rent a roller rink for a few hours. When considering the theme or decor of the event you should always do your best to make it personal. If you will be doing a life celebration you may want to make it personal with the person's favorite flowers for the centerpieces or make their favorite foods/snacks for the celebration. I think you get the jest of it.. Picking the theme and deciding the decor is my favorite part! You get to be as creative as you would like… or if that's too overwhelming don't worry the internet has a TON of places and ideas you can research. If you have a very tight budget, the Dollar Tree or 99 cent store has some great finds, in addition they have excellent options for glassware if you are looking to make a candy table or vases for centerpieces. I also enjoy Orientaltrading.com for bulk items and for party favors. There are numerous ideas for instance, a puppet show, laser tag, swim party, fashion show, candy party, even a spa party. Whatever you can envision you can make possible.

Picking the date is essential. You need to consider a few things when you choose a date. Do your best to not pick a date on a holiday (depending on the event) most people have plans already established for surrounding holidays. Of course a Christmas party would be planned closer to Christmas but not on Christmas Eve or day unless that is something that is already determined with your guests.

A quick tip, I don't recommend a date that clashes with another party of a family member or a friend, that probably won't go over too well. You also want to think about the time of year and what the weather will be like. Nobody likes going to a party where they are sitting in 100 degree heat sweating bullets with no shade or when it's 40 degrees outside and there are no heaters or no place to go inside and get warm.

This brings us to the invite portion. If you are planning a wedding or a formal affair you will need to send out the "Save the Date" 12 weeks prior to the event and the actual invites go out 8 weeks before the wedding with an RSVP date within 4 weeks of the event, this gives you enough time to make your seating arrangements (if you choose to do so) and to give a more concise number of guests to your venue coordinator. When it comes to a casual event sending out the invites is best 4-6 weeks prior to the event with an RSVP date within 2 weeks of the event. Ok, so now you've got the bones of the event planned, let's keep going!

3

# What Drink Is That?

This chapter will be dedicated to food, drinks and desserts. When deciding on what to serve at the event there are a lot of factors to take into consideration. First, what kind of event is it? Is it casual or lavish? Is it extravagant or thrifty? It may even be a potluck which is also fabulous. Regardless of which way you go, it is imperative that you consider the amount of people that are coming and how much money you want to spend on feeding your guests. We all know about the dreaded "chicken dinner" at weddings which sometimes is out of the hosts control. It may be the lesser of two evils. Nonetheless if you are restricted to the chicken dinner you can always add other things from the menu or even hire a separate caterer to make something special that stands out as a side dish. I think when people go to weddings they expect that the food will be mid to fair because when you are serving so many people it can get quite expensive. That is not to say that there are no venues that have outstanding food, it's just that it is usually the minority and not the majority. And to be honest most people are not at weddings for the food they are there to spend time with friends and family and have a fantastic time. At the end of the day as humans we enjoy spending quality time together especially if it is celebrating love.

When it comes to your less lavish events such as a birthday party or a retirement party etc..you can absolutely do the cooking yourself (if the event is at a controlled location IE…your house) or maybe you choose to hold the event at a restaurant then you will know exactly what to expect for taste, this option is much easier and one less thing for you to worry about however it will cost you quite a bit more. Regardless, your meal choices should always have options for the kids, vegetarians or any other dietary restrictions. When figuring out the portion size you can estimate that each adult will eat 1 lb of food and children will eat ½ lb. A quick tip, people will always eat more in the evening than in the daytime.

When it comes to serving the meal the timing is crucial. Avoid serving meals too early or too late. You want to make sure that your guests have enough time to enjoy their food before doing something else. When doing a buffet, arrange the food to what seems most logical with starters, main dish then sides and lastly desserts. Have the serving tables open on both sides so guests do not get congested when dishing their plates. I touched on this a bit before but be poignant about keeping hot foods hot, and cold foods cold. Use chafing dishes or a warming tray for hot foods and ice baths or ice buffets for cold foods.

Pay attention to the presentation of the food. We are visual creatures we pick and choose based on a large portion of what we see and smell. Although a dish may be delicious if it does not look or smell appetizing more times than not it will be skipped over (which equals wasting food/money.)

If you will be hosting an outdoor party you have to take into consideration the weather and the insects. I do have a great go-to for the flies. I will post it in my Tips and Tricks chapter at the end of the book. If it is a warmer time of year you want to make sure that whatever food you put out will not spoil in the warm heat. I would recommend an inflatable serving bar for fruits and veggies or anything that you want to keep cool in the summer heat. In the winter time it is best to serve items that are more cozy and comfort foods for example macaroni and cheese or even a pot of chicken tortilla soup. Both of those are super yummy and economical and easy to make and they will feed many. Chips and salsa are ALWAYS a big hit with guests and if you wanted to kick it up you could even do fresh guacamole!

A clever idea when having to feed many people on a budget is to be sure to put out foods that guests can snack on prior to eating the main dish, so they are not starving when it comes time to eat the main meal. For example, for my kids' birthday parties and even BBQ's I will set up a nachos bar. I will have fresh tortilla chips, nacho cheese, chili, fresh grated cheese, jalapenos, sour cream, and some chives so that guests can help themselves while waiting for the BBQ to be ready. Just to be clear when people go to parties they will be hungry and will expect to eat fairly soon upon arrival. So it is important that you have some sort of appetizers, snacks or munchies for them.

For casual events something as simple as the American "go to" hamburgers are always an excellent economical choice. If you want it a little spruced up you can make a hamburger bar where the options can include veggie or turkey burgers. You can have bacon, swiss cheese, Ortega chili's, onion straws, bourbon mayo etc… Really anything you can think of that would be amazing on a burger and to make it cute you can put out a little sign that says "Build Your Own Burger" You can even make french fries or sweet potato fries and don't forget to put out the pickles ….and of course chips and any kind of macaroni salad is always a hit! Remember people like options, and they like to be able to put what they like on their plate.

One of my favorite "go to" ideas for food is hiring a taco guy. Now it may not be as economical as doing hamburgers and hot dogs but you can guarantee that just about everyone will enjoy that option. If you need to make up the money elsewhere you can always go cheaper on drinks or decorations to make up the difference in cost. Regardless if you go economical or even catered you just want to be positive to have enough food for everyone to get full and feel satisfied. The last thing you want people to be talking about is how there "wasn't enough food" yikes!

MAY THE FRUIT
BE WITH YOU!

In regards to the drinks depending on the event, if it is a formal event the venue will serve their options for drinks and most likely will have a bar with some cocktails that you will have agreed upon with your event coordinator. As you may know with weddings in the past the trendy thing to do was to have a "signature drink" but now the popular thing to do is have a "secret cocktail menu." To do this you can put a special mark or symbol on the ceremony program and show it to the bartender and he/she will know exactly what that means or you have a designated friend order the cocktail and it will be so beautifully garnished and everyone will be asking, "WHAT DRINK IS THAT?" The cocktail should bear the name of something that is special about the bride and groom like their first date, or their favorite restaurant. I love this idea, it sounds so fun!

When having a casual birthday party or a common event the most cost effective way to serve drinks would be to have a few 1-2 gallon beverage dispensers. One can be used for lemon or cucumber water and the other can be pink lemonade or iced tea. You can also have a few coolers with other options available to your guests. Be sure to place a tag on each cooler describing what kind of drinks are in the cooler. This is especially important if you are going to be serving adult drinks. Your event should have enough options that if someone does not want to drink soda or alcohol they don't have to or if they only prefer clear or decaf sodas they have that option as well.

When it comes to the dessert for an event the possibilities are endless, of course for your formal events you will contract out to your favorite bakery or the venue will supply you with a bakery they work with. You will do some cake tasting and get to choose your cake flavors, your frosting and your style of cake. Some people choose to have another dessert in addition to their wedding cake. That is completely acceptable and if you have the money in the budget feel free to go hog wild!!

Regarding the standard type of parties, less and less people are opting for cake. Or some will do a small cake specifically for the occasion and will also do cupcakes. Cupcakes are easier to pass around with less mess. They also make cupcake cakes which I'm sure you've seen before. Furthermore, an alternative idea is having a "no frosting" cake, where the cake has little to no frosting but will be adorned with fruits instead. But as we all know kids love to lick the frosting off of a cupcake or a piece of cake so it simply is just a preference. In some instances people will opt for other options for desserts such as pies, caramel apples or brownies, or even hot fudge sundaes… the list goes on and on. The dessert options are endless and 100% up to you and your budget.

Don't be afraid or intimated to be creative and make your own pastries. Many people are quite talented at making their own treats, like a fruit trifle, cake pops, lemon bars or even tiramisu. Either way your guests are going to be overjoyed and eager to delight in your homemade goodies. When I realized how expensive designer cakes were becoming, I started to order my cakes from the grocery store. I would pick the basic design and colors, my flavors and style and when I would bring it home I would add all my extra decorations on it. Depending on the theme I would add flowers or a Barbie doll and butterflies etc…It made my cakes look so much more personal and fancy. .

# 4

# It's Time to Party…

Choosing the right entertainment for your event can be tricky.. Whether you pick a DJ or a band it is imperative that you do your homework and research to pick the best people for the job. For a formal event I would highly recommend that you interview a number of DJs or get one referred to you by someone you trust. The same with the live music, hopefully you have heard them before and know that they are what you are looking for. You need to make sure your contracts are very detailed and have exactly what is to be expected of them regarding set up and break down time, and the times they will be playing or DJing so there is no confusion. You also want to have an idea of a set list. Be mindful of your audience, formal wedding guests may not want to listen to "gangster rap" or maybe they do… you just need to go over these details with a fine tooth comb.

In addition this part of the planning can be costly, DJs and bands have different price points so you will need to be sure to stay within your budget. Whether you choose to use a DJ or a band or maybe a mariachi band the music will dictate the vibe of the event. Make sure that the music choices give you the emotion and the energy you are wanting.

Another great idea for a kids party is a game truck or even an escape room game truck. My son and all his friends had an amazing time with the game truck I rented. He didn't stop talking about that one for a while. Cha Ching....mom scored big points!!! We did a movie night once where I bought a giant movie screen and a projector and I made popcorn and bought lots of candy from the Dollar Tree and every one got a homemade ticket when they arrived and before the movie started they were able to get a bag of popcorn and pick 2 candies. I made a makeshift concession stand and my daughter worked behind the counter. She took tickets and handed out popcorn and candy, it really was a big hit. Entertainment can be anything that coincides with the theme of the party and plays a role in the party.

With some parties you may have special guests like a princess or a certain superhero show up. The kids always get a kick out of seeing their favorite character in real life. Normally these special guests will run you anywhere from $200-$500 depending on how long and how many guests you have. For one of my daughters' parties I had a fairy come, she sang and played games with the kids and gave all of my daughters friends a special treat bag.

My daughter absolutely loved it! Once for a unicorn party I rented some "unicorns" from a company I found online and the kids all got to have their turn riding one. Of course there are your typical jumpers which the little kids always enjoy and for older kids having a photo booth is guaranteed to make them smile.

When considering entertainment options be sure that the logistics make sense.  For example, If you want to have a mechanical bull, you will need to be positive that you have enough room to house the set up. Some of these machines can be quite large. In addition mechanical bulls usually require 1 specific person to pass out wavers and control the machine. You may want to have a back-up or contingency plan in place for any unforeseen circumstances this can include the weather. Sometimes the weather does not cooperate with our plans.

For adult entertainment you can have a poker party where tables are set up and you hire a company to run the tables just like a casino. You can also do a painting party, where you hire a commissioned artist to come set up and show everyone how to paint a specific scene.

You can serve hors d'oeuvres, with wine or non-alcoholic drinks. The exciting thing about this idea is that everyone gets to take home something they have made. Another playful idea is hosting a cooking class. This is a fantastic approach to getting everyone involved and engaged. Maybe you have some single friends that you want to set up, having a theme that requires hands on is a fantastic idea. It serves as a way for guests to get to know each other better and have some solid laughs.

As long as you are paying attention to your audience demographics, understanding who are your age groups, and their interests and preferences you will do just fine. In addition, be sure to be conscious of cultural backgrounds and the diversity of your guests. Make sure you employ reputable and professional performers and entertainers. Be sure to check references and reviews. Keep in mind that you want to make the experience a memorable one for your guests and that it leaves a lasting impression.

When the event is over you may want to pass out a gift bag or a party favor as a keepsake to your guests. Providing a gift bag or a favor is a thoughtful gesture and serves as a sign of gratitude for your guests attending your event. Depending on the event the favor can be big or small. There really is no right or wrong, it can be a useful item such as a personalized bottle opener or a wine stopper. It can be filled with sweet goodies like chocolates or hard candy. You could even do a handmade item made from a local artisan. You can add a custom made sticker with a "Thank You For Coming" to personalize it.

For formal events I have seen all kinds of terrific ideas. For instance some people do personalized candy or tiny bubbles, and key chains. I'm sure you have received some yourself. Whichever idea you go with, make sure you choose an attractive bag. Be aware to not overspend on your favor/gift bag budget. See to it that the package is durable and won't easily break, make sure that all the spelling is correct and keep the design of the gift bag simple. And of course do not forget to verbally give a thank you as guests are leaving with stuffed tummies, loads of memories, and full hearts. I can guarantee that they will look forward to your next shindig!

# 5

# Tips and Tricks

- Fly swatter fans, for outdoor events - Amazon link https://a.co/d/7L85svN
- For swim parties be sure to have plenty of towels, sunscreen and toys available
- To keep plastic tablecloths from flying off take the 2 corners and tie in a knot under table
- Centerpieces should be either 12 inches and shorter OR 24 inches and higher
- Take pictures before event begins, once event starts you will be too busy
- Not all centerpieces need to match, you can mix and match centerpieces
- The Rule of 3 -if you're displaying a similar set of decor, use 3 different sizes placed near each other eg…candlesticks or candles
- To make up empty space in a flower centerpiece use fuller greens such as eucalyptus and baby's breath
- For a formal event you should always have a "survival kit"

it should include band aids, sunscreen, bobby pins, Tylenol or Motrin, sharpie, phone charger, tissues, and safety pins and straight pins

- Inflatable serving bar for cold foods - Amazon link https://a .co/d/1sXfCA2
- Make sure you have enough food or meals for your staff/helpers eg., bartenders, and photographer
- Anticipate the needs of your guests
- Buy your own helium tank and make your own balloon designs
- Be able to adapt to unexpected changes
- Pay exceptional attention to detail, remember the devils in the details

# 6

# Conclusion

These are the basic requirements for a successful event from beginning to end. There is a lot more meat and potatoes to get into but I believe you get the fundamentals of planning an event. I hope you enjoyed my quick and easy handbook. Thankfully we have a wealth of knowledge at our fingertips with the internet being so accessible for any questions or for any research you want to do. My wish is that you gained some knowledge and confidence about hosting your next event.

Really, all we really want is to have an incredible day or evening with those we love and cherish the most. Our dream is to have memories that will last a lifetime, because in the end all we have are the lasting impressions and moments of our time together. So Good Luck to you, and Cheers to your next amazing event!

# About the Author

I'm a married mom of 2 amazing kiddos. My kids really are my life and they are the reason I started this journey to begin with. My husband is the love of my life and the best partner ever, we make a great team. We live in California with our 4 rescue pups who are all spoiled rotten. I have many passions in life like reading, rescuing dogs, and having a healthy lifestyle but event planning has always taken a front seat. I look forward to all birthday celebrations and holidays and even when there is no reason for a party we will still find a way to have one!